INDIE AUTHOR CONFIDENTIAL 13

SECRETS NO ONE WILL TELL YOU ABOUT BEING A WRITER

M.L. RONN

Cover Design by Pixelstudio.

Cover Art by jasoshulwathon.

Editing by BZ Hercules.

Time Period Covered in This Book: Q2 2023

Special thank you to the following people on Patreon who supported this book: Matty Dalrymple, BB Dee, Michael Guishard, Jon Howard, Sheila Klein, Olivia Williams, and Ryan Zee.

Some links in this book contain affiliate links. If you purchase books and services through these links, I receive a small commission at no cost to you. You are under no obligation to use these links, but thank you if you do!

For more helpful writing tips and advice, subscribe to the Author Level Up YouTube channel: www.youtube.com/authorlevelup.

CONTENTS

ABOUT THIS SERIES

This isn't your typical writing self-help book. This series is a compilation of lessons learned from an indie author trying to walk the path to success. Follow author M.L. Ronn (Michael La Ronn) as he navigates what it means to master the craft of writing, marketing, and running a profitable publishing business. Learn from his successes and failures, and learn about things that most successful authors only talk about behind the scenes.

To read all the collected volumes of this series in an anthology, visit www.authorlevelup.com/confidential.

INTRODUCTION

This volume is about getting back on track. As I will discuss in the first chapter of this volume, I suffered a temporary debilitating illness in the middle of this quarter that rendered my progress toward my goals almost null. The recovery took me approximately ten weeks, representing most of the quarter. However, I still made progress, and I will document the progress I did make. I also had some big wins this quarter despite my setback.

That's the thing about running a business that lasts your entire lifetime; sometimes, you will have periods of great growth and advancement; other times, you will have periods of stalling, and the rest of the time will be somewhere in between.

Despite being out of commission for a long time this quarter, I never once forgot that I own my copyrights for my entire life plus 70 years. That's an extremely long time, and not being productive for one quarter isn't going to kill me. I look back on this quarter and probably not even remember it in a few years. Therefore, I didn't beat myself up too much.

In the Become a Writing Master section, I discuss lessons learned from my medical setback, how I stayed minimally productive, and a people-watching session at a lake shortly after my recovery.

In the Become a Technology and Data-Driven Writer section, I discuss investing in a new computer, building an ONIX data feed, and a strategy I refined to finally conquer my to-do list once and for all.

In the Looking Forward section, I discuss a new marketing strategy I'd like to try, beating Parkinson's Law, and creating a new speaking setup while on the road.

In any case, I hope you enjoy this volume, and I hope it teaches an important lesson: even when you are unproductive, you can still be productive!

--M.L. Ronn
    Des Moines, Iowa
    July 16, 2023

BECOME A WRITING MASTER

WHAT MOLD POISONING
TAUGHT ME

In one of my worst setbacks of the year, I caught mold poisoning in a hotel room.

This is a long story that I won't go into as it is complicated as to why I contracted mold poisoning and why I even stayed at this hotel in the first place. But suffice it to say, an unfortunate series of events occurred, and I found myself experiencing severe asthma, shortness of breath, and a stuffy nose that promptly went away the moment I relocated from this hotel. To make matters more unfortunate, this was an upscale hotel chain that enjoys a sterling reputation.

Anyway, the entire episode set me back ten weeks. I had to go to the doctor, who recommended seeking hyperbaric oxygen treatment. In this treatment style, you lie in an oxygen chamber for an hour as it pressurizes the air around you, and you breathe pure oxygen through an oxygen mask. I had to do this twice a week. Even simple things like taking my dog on a walk or a jogging on a treadmill were challenging. I feared the damage would be permanent, but the doctors confirmed there was no mold in my lungs, and my symptoms would last a few weeks at best to a few months at worst. I started to feel better around the six-week mark. It was hard to concentrate, work, and, most importantly, write, but I did my best in short bursts of energy. For these reasons, my productivity this quarter was at a record low.

I had to step away from my writing business for a short time. The beauty of running an independent publishing business is that my books kept selling. My email list kept converting, and opportunities kept knocking, even though I was technically out of commission.

That's why I love publishing. How many professionals can say that the business continues even when they aren't working?

Once I started feeling better, I assessed everything that needed to be done and planned to catch up, which I did over a month.

Now I am back to my regular schedule, and it feels good to be back. But it also feels good to stop and reflect on my progress too.

While I wouldn't recommend mold poisoning to my worst enemies, I am grateful for the lessons it taught me. I took care of myself, and now I can move forward.

KEEPING THE "WRITING SHIP" AFLOAT DURING HARD TIMES

I mentioned in a previous chapter that I had to step away from my writing for a short time this year. In doing so, I had to let some things go, but others ran themselves with minimal intervention. I want to document some of the successes and failures in this chapter so that I can refer to them in the future. They may also be helpful to someone else reading this.

Beating Parkinson's Law

I'll discuss "Beating Parkinson's Law" later in this volume. However, I spent time finishing some projects ahead of schedule even though I didn't have to: magazine articles, presentation slides for speaking engagements, and so on. By doing that, I avoided several deadlines that would have come due during my rest period. These deadlines would have increased my stress level considerably.

I didn't know at the time that finishing these projects early was going to help me, but I'm glad I finished them when I did. This is one major reason I'll discuss Parkinson's Law later.

Consuming Content

Though I stepped away, I never stopped reading and consuming content. I read novels and nonfiction books, and I watched many documentaries and YouTube videos. I continued to write down story ideas as they came to me. This kept my brain "lubricated," making my transition back into writing much easier.

Emails

Emails are the beating heart of my writing business. Almost every opportunity that comes my way--good or bad--begins as an email. For example, speaking opportunities begin as emails. So do podcast and blog interviews. On the contrary, if something is wrong on my website, readers email me about it. You get the idea.

With a few notable exceptions that I have documented throughout this series, I am usually pretty good about managing my email. Most emails that hit my inbox receive a response within 24 hours or less. During times of illness or extenuating circumstances, my worst-case response time is around five days, which is also decent.

In prioritizing emails while I stepped away, I made sure to address the following types of emails immediately:

- emails from organizers regarding speaking engagements that I already agreed to
- emails from organizers regarding speaking engagements that I had not yet agreed to (so I could give them quick declinations)
- emails from retailers advising of a problem with one of my books
- emails from writer friends in my inner circle
- emails from fans

Everything else received a lower priority. I got to it when I got to it, usually between one and five days, during times when I had enough energy and time to respond.

Fortunately, I didn't receive any complaints or emails from people following up a second time, so it is clear that this emergency procedure worked well.

By strategically prioritizing my email inbox, I believe I eliminated many potential problems that could have arisen while stepping away for so long.

Book Production

Book production is also another critical part of my writing business. Without books, I would have no career. However, *not* writing helped me in a few ways:

- it lowered my expenses, and
- it allowed me to focus strictly on issues with my backlist

Not having to worry about front-list titles was very helpful.

It would have been unfavorable to step away during a book launch or a major marketing campaign. The timing just happened to work out this time, but I'll have to keep this in mind in the future.

Automation

Automation is another critical part of my writing. In the *Indie Author Confidential* series, I've thoroughly detailed my adventures and escapades in this area. Little things like automated email rules, WordPress plugins, utility tools on my computer, and more added up in a big way. For example, I needed to find a receipt during a dispute with a vendor; because I was well organized and used the right tools, what would have taken the average person at least 30 minutes took me two.

Not Beating Myself Up

I didn't feel bad for stepping away. I didn't lament all the words I couldn't write. I just took it easy. That helped me tremendously because it took the pressure off.

Anyway, those were a few of the strategies that helped me succeed even though I had to take time away this year. In the grand scheme of things, I will reflect on these unproductive weeks...and probably not remember much about them.

LESSONS FROM THE MAN FROM ST. PETERSBURG

There are novels, and then there are novels' novels. *The Man from St. Petersburg* by Ken Follett is one of the latter. I read this for the first time and was blown away by it. It's an example of a master at work. I immediately reread the book because I was so captivated by it. So many fantastic moments serve as excellent illustrations of exactly how to pull off certain literary techniques on the page.

That's why I love reading the works of mega-bestsellers. They're such masters of their craft that they make it look easy. It's like watching a professional public speaker like Les Brown or Zig Ziglar. They have practiced to the point where the speaking is natural, and they can communicate so simply. I've learned that the simpler writing appears, the more mastery you can find.

In this chapter, I'll recap my major lessons from *The Man from St. Petersburg*. Warning that there are spoilers in this chapter. They can't be avoided.

A Coincidence in Any Other Hands

. . .

Story-wise, I enjoyed *The Man from St. Petersburg* immensely, but there are some very strange coincidences that I don't think readers would put up with if the author weren't Ken Follett.

For example, the main character Feliks is an antihero who, early in his life, has an affair with a noblewoman who is sent away to England as punishment. He then becomes an anarchist and decides to kill the nephew of the tzar, who happens to be in England on diplomatic business. The nephew just so happens to be staying with none other than the very woman he had an affair with back in Russia.

The coincidences are a little too much, but the characters were so great that it didn't matter. This novel taught me that character development is everything. It makes up for all other deficiencies in a novel.

Infusion of Opinion with the Five Senses

There are many moments in the novel when Follett does an incredible job painting a scene using the five senses through the eyes of the viewpoint character, but he takes it a step further. Often, he infuses the sense with a character's *opinion* about the setting.

In the opening scene, for example, one of the main characters is relaxing at home on a peaceful afternoon. Sensory details include a willow tree with a "head of girlish curls" and "contented bees" buzzing around the yard. These images match the character's mindset. What an amazing tip.

In another scene, the main character has just met a daughter he didn't know he had. The next morning, the only thing he can fixate on is children. The next morning, he can only fixate on children. He notices them everywhere in his apartment building. Each sense is tied to something a child is doing, reminding him of his daughter.

There are many more examples, but I learned that it's not enough just to describe a scene in the five senses. Whenever possible, you should also infuse the senses with the character's opinion of the setting. It's a subconscious touch that helps the reader stay engaged and enthralled in the story.

I do this, but not often enough—I need to be more intentional about it. It really works wonders in a scene.

The Simplicity of Human Desires

To the point of being almost too generic, I'll say that Follett draws on basic human desires in this story to great effect.

The antihero Feliks is driven by ideology and the need for violence as purification. He wants to start a revolution in Russia.

The hero Walden is driven by the desire to serve England and to marshal Russia's help with the war against Germany. He is also driven by love for his wife, who does not love him back.

Walden's wife, Lydia, is driven by shame and passion around her affair with Feliks.

Walden's daughter, Charlotte, is driven by ideals for suffragism, which gets her into trouble and precipitates her meeting Feliks, who turns out to be her father. She is also a typical teenager and rebels against her parents.

These desires are all too human. You could almost call these stereotypical tropes. I suppose human desires drive every fictional character to an extent, but it's so in-your-face in this novel. It might put some people off, but I loved it.

. . .

An Antihero Anchor

Feliks is a compelling antihero, possibly one of the best I've ever read. I will be returning to his chapters whenever I need guidance or inspiration on how to write an antihero. I will return to his chapters whenever I need guidance or inspiration on writing an antihero.

He's an antihero that you root for. In many ways, Follett treats him like a hero but with demented goals. People often say that "villains are heroes with reverse character development," but that's not the case here. Feliks grows and develops over the course of the novel, even though his end goal is evil. Perhaps antiheroes should be treated the same way as regular heroes.

Final Thoughts

I wish I had been better positioned to study *The Man from St. Petersburg* when I read it, but I think my subconscious absorbed everything I needed to learn. I am grateful for reading it because it kept my mind entertained and active while I was on a hiatus this quarter.

SHARPENING MY WRITER'S EYE AT LAKE MONONA

Near the end of my recovery, I traveled to Madison, Wisconsin, for work, and my family tagged along with me. We visited Lake Monona, a small freshwater drainage lake just south of the state capital. While there, I felt the old "writer's inspiration" taking hold—these are periods when my gut tells me to pay attention to everything around me because it could end up in a novel one day. I've learned to listen to instinct during those times, so I kept my phone out and took notes on almost everything I saw.

Overall, it was a fun exercise, making me want to go people-watching more frequently. I'm including my notes here. As with all my notes, I captured the area in the five senses.

Sight

- Glimmers of phosphorescence on the water, scattering like stars in the cosmos
- Water surface marked by rippling lattices, like a fretwork of crests and troughs

- Invisible hands kneading the water
- Waves billowing like curtains, tossed about by the lake's breath
- Waves etching intricate argyle patterns on their crests
- Shiny granite-colored rocks glimpsed between the capricious waves, reminiscent of an aquarium's scenery
- Monumental rocks lining the waterfront, meticulously set as if sculpted by divine hands
- Speedboat leaving an ultramarine wake behind the boat
- Seagulls in a macabre ballet circling a skeletal tree
- Algae bloom bouncing on the water's surface like confetti
- A carpet of dead grass, lost beneath the tyranny of overgrown weeds
- A ten-year-old girl in an orange life vest learning how to ski, clinging to a boat's edge
- The frothy waves appear like clusters of animated bubbles
- A chiaroscuro of tree and leaf shadows, adding an oscillating pattern over the dead grass
- An elusive white moth prancing over the foliage
- A couple immortalizing the moment at a pebbly beach with a series of selfies
- The sky, an artist's gradient, azure above the lake, fading into a wash of white and yellow over the lake houses hidden by slanted trees
- A boat with a red canvas top, swaying like it's battling the lake's whim
- Blinding sunlight seeping through the gaps in the trees

- Sunlight piercing through the insect-bitten leaves, creating a natural stained glass effect
- A mahogany picnic table stained by bird droppings
- Seagulls gracefully skim the water's surface, dancing with the ripples
- The erratic flight path of a seagull, a ragged circle around the beach, and the waves
- A circle of seagulls, broken occasionally by individual paths
- A stark warning sign about invasive species, an advisory for people to scrutinize their boats
- Beach towels in a riot of colors, and Green Bay Packers camping chairs proudly on display
- A pontoon boat with a gravel-laden wooden top, leisurely spinning in place
- Jumbo gas cans stationed on a metal pier
- A man doing a leisurely backstroke, creating ripples in his wake
- A grim sign warning about the lake's fish being dirty, an advisory to limit consumption
- An easel board advertising a waterski show at 6 PM
- A man in wired earbuds, sunglasses, and a white baseball cap sitting on a camping chair, engrossed in his phone
- Hackberry leaves with their dagger-like contours, occasionally resembling sea drops
- A lone floss pick in the dirt
- Weeds like green streaks on a canvas of sepia
- An earthy palette of baked wheat
- Snaking tree roots, like the ghastly fingers of the departed clawing through the earth
- Cars solar shades glinting from inside windshields

- A French-inspired restaurant with billowing awnings, globe lamps shimmering, and flower troughs hosting a vibrant spectrum of flowers

Smell

- A subtle marine scent laced with a hint of saline
- The acidic stench of seagull poop

Sound

-

- Rhythmic lapping of water against the rocks
- The casual hum of passing cars
- The rhythmic thump of joggers
- An insectoid hum of speeding bicycles on a bike path that traces itself along the shore
- Bicycle chains grinding like mechanical insects engaged in a choral symphony
- Seagulls honking
- Cars bereft of mufflers, roaring like irate hornets
- Snatches of overheard conversations—someone talking about a sixth sense, another talking about their plans for the evening
- Loud music reverberating from subwoofers
- Squawking pandemonium as seagulls and ducks squabble over scraps of fried chicken
- Gravel underfoot, crunching, scuffing, gleaming, a testament to its rugged journey

- Waves growling at the shore, splashing with enthusiasm, lapping with a gentle whisper

Feel

- Cool summer breeze interspersed with the sun's fiery kiss
- A wooden dock, an unstable dance floor, rocking back and forth underfoot

BECOME A TECHNOLOGY
AND DATA-DRIVEN WRITER

INVESTING IN A TRAVELING
WRITING COMPUTER

In the last volume of this series, I talked about my adventures with renting a Mac in the cloud. While not perfect, it helped me stay minimally productive while on the road and it helped me overcome some unfortunate shortcomings with my decade-old MacBook Air computer.

However, thinking about this solution, I realized it was a fool's errand. I couldn't run the applications I needed, and there were many barriers. Also, there were other roadblocks that made renting a Mac in the cloud undesirable, such as having to log in with a complicated username and password every time I wanted to use the rented Mac.

I did some research and decided that I was willing to spend money to help me solve this problem. I would be traveling almost every other month in 2023, and I needed a real solution, not a quick fix.

My choices were:

- Purchase another Mac or an iPad as my "road" computer.

- Purchase a Windows laptop or tablet as my "road" computer.

During my research, I identified my key priority: I needed to be able to dictate and transcribe my work on the go. This was the most important thing. I could accomplish almost every other need in my writing business on any operating system, with the exception of formatting my books in Vellum, which would have to be accomplished through renting a Mac in the cloud if I purchased a Windows computer.

I ruled out a Mac computer because I didn't want to spend the money on one. They're expensive, and too much for a computer that I would only use when traveling.

I also ruled out an iPad because 1) iPads because they are glorified iPhones, 2) you can't operate an iPad as a computer, and its operating system is far from an actual operating system, and 3) iPad (and Macs, for that matter) don't provide a reliable dictation solution.

Therefore, I settled on Windows. I find that the current generation of Windows laptops is very expensive and slightly overpriced for what you get. I think the tablet offerings are much better. I ultimately settled on a Microsoft Surface Pro 10 for the following reasons:

- It can run Dragon.
- It can run Microsoft Office well.

The Surface products are not cheap, but they are cheaper than Mac computers. As I waited for the computer to arrive, I started getting buyer's remorse. All signs of the remorse disappeared, however, when the tablet arrived. It was easy to set up, immensely portable, and it delivered excellent performance. I tested it on my first trip and it performed extremely well, allowing me to perform 95 percent of the tasks I needed to. Not only could I write my books, browse the internet, and check my emails with a full screen and keyboard, but I could also accomplish other miscellaneous tasks that I couldn't do previously on my phone, such as updating a cover in Photoshop or accessing miscellaneous project files such as my sales database. I receive so many emails and have so many projects in the works that miscellaneous tasks frequently arise when I'm on the road. I also occasionally need to do a podcast interview on the road as well. The Surface helped me accomplish all of that and more.

It also helped me become more knowledgeable about the Windows operating system. I consider myself to be what you would call ambidextrous with operating systems. I am equally adept at Windows and MacOS, but I know Mac computers slightly better. By having a native Windows machine, I can explore the Windows world more. There is a lot to like about Windows 11, for example.

I recognize that I'm fortunate to have the resources to purchase a secondary device. I just wanted to share how this helped me level off and remain productive while on the road.

BUILDING AN ONIX DATA FEED

I achieved a signature accomplishment this quarter that harkens back to the very first volume of this series.

In the inaugural volume of *Indie Author Confidential,* I wrote a chapter called "ONIX, Metadata, and Databases." In that chapter, I wrote:

"I have a subscription to LinkedIn Learning and happened to encounter a course on metadata and book publishing.

The course was like the Matrix. It validated all of my database work. It turns out that traditional publishers also manage their books in databases. They use an industry-standard markup language called ONIX, which stands for Online Information Exchange. An ONIX file contains all of a book's or books' metadata and stores it in a special format so that publishers can, with a click of a button, send their books to distributors, retailers, bookstores, and other trading partners.

I always thought there was some poor soul at a publishing house who had to upload and manage the publishers' books on various dashboards. That's not how it works, at least for large publishers.

ONIX is generally exclusive to traditional publishing circles, but the truth is that indie authors can use it too.

In fact, the book database I developed was a crude version of ONIX without realizing it.

Then I discovered through the course that there is professional metadata management software that was designed to help publishers manage this problem. It costs less than $100 (at the time of this writing).

That's when I realized: why develop my own format when I can use the industry standard?

By adopting the industry standard, I can integrate a future database more easily with my website and also bulk upload my titles to a future retailer without any additional effort.

Learning about ONIX was a critical step in my database journey."

My learnings in this previous chapter helped me in ways I couldn't imagine. In the last volume, I discussed my travels to Saudi Arabia. There, I connected with the nonprofit Benetech, who serves the blind and low-sighted community by advocating for better accessibility in publishing. I received an invitation to donate my books to Bookshare, their database of books for their community. Bookshare provides these books at low-cost, and they have an app that is designed to help people with visibility barriers read easier. There is a shortage of science fiction and fantasy in the database.

Reaching these readers was a no-brainer, but there was one drawback: I had to donate my books through an ONIX data feed. The Bookshare team sent me instructions on how to upload my ONIX file.

Good thing I learned about ONIX and had familiarity with it. I pulled out my notes from 2020 when I had my first adventure learning about ONIX. I downloaded the leading ONIX app, ONIXEdit, which will cost me approximately $150 per year. I immediately got to work building my ONIX feed, which was a database very similar to the one I built myself in 2020.

Keeping in mind all the database best practices I've learned, I built a working, validating, metadata-rich ONIX feed in about two days. My master publishing file helped tremendously because I had all my metadata in one place. The clipboard manager tool I use also saved me an unbelievable amount of time because I didn't have to copy and paste data a gazillion times.

The process of preparing an ONIX feed contained the following steps:

- Reformatting my books to achieve current accessibility best practices such as ePub 3.0, alt tags for all images, properly sequenced headers, and so on
- Gathering the metadata for my books and using it to create the ONIX feed
- Preparing the ebook and cover files
- Validating that my books were transmitted properly

Reformatting My Books

Before embarking on this project, my ebooks were all ePUB 2.0. Accessibility best practices require ePUB 3.0, so I had to reformat everything. Fortunately, this wasn't too hard because I just had to "regenerate" the books in Vellum.

I have an internal method of tracking versions on my books, so once I regenerated everything, I had to update my "change logs," which have the version and date I regenerated each book.

This helps me keep everything organized and documented. Also, I put the version number in the copyright page of my books so I can tell which version of the book is published by looking at the retailer sample on the sales page.

Finally, I had to validate the new ePUB 3.0 books using an ePUB checker as well as Ace+ by Daisy. I did a couple books as a test run and found some minor issues that needed to be addressed, mostly by tweaking a setting in Vellum. The biggest culprit was forgetting to put alt tags on a few rogue images.

Again, not hard, but time-consuming.

Gathering the Metadata for My Books

I mentioned that I used my master publishing file and my clipboard manager app.

The master publishing file contained all of the data I needed to populate the ONIX feed, such as title, subtitle, ISBN, and more. The only field my master publishing file did not contain was the book description. When I adopted my clipboard manager last year, I pre-emptively saved *all* of my book descriptions into the manager because I knew I would need them often. I can access any book description with a keyboard shortcut and a quick search. Oh man, that was a game changer!

I populated the metadata fields quickly. All I had to do afterward was double-check the data entry.

Preparing the Ebook and Cover Files

.   .   .

To submit my files, I had to submit an ePUB and a JPEG file with the ISBN as the filename. Not hard—just time-consuming.

I don't know if this is the case for every vendor that accepts ONIX, but you have to submit the ONIX XML file *in addition* to the ePUB and the cover. You also have to submit them via an FTP server. Fortunately, I also have prior experience with FTPs. I geeked out on FTPs in high school during a brief stint as a video game music journalist for a major game review site—I received free VGM albums to review via FTP servers.

Once it was time to submit my files, I said a prayer, uploaded the books, and hoped for the best.

The next morning, all of the books were available for Bookshare readers. All of my books passed their validation procedures and there were no technical hang ups. I nailed it on my first try. Wow!

Ever since, I have submitted books and they show up within hours. Say what you want about ONIX—yes, it's clunky, and no, it's not sexy--but it works, and when it works, it's kind of amazing. Whether you have one book or 1,000, you can publish them all in one click.

This is precisely the type of efficiency I have dreamed of. Imagine a new retailer in the future where I can simply submit an ONIX feed and be done, instead of submitting each book manually.

Now that I have a working, validated ONIX feed, I can port it to any retailer that will accept it. Will that ever happen? I don't know, but it's still a level up.

Validating My Books

. . .

Once my books were published, I did a quick round of QA to ensure that everything was loaded properly. Other than a minor HTML with my book descriptions, everything looked good and met my personal standards.

Anyway ,I'm proud of this accomplishment. The experience taught me a great deal about how traditional publishers use ONIX. It also help me coalesce the myriad skills I've learned throughout my career, and it was fun to test myself to see how well I truly learned them.

I have a hunch that this won't be the last time I write about ONIX...

CONQUERING MY TO-DO LIST...
FINALLY

I have struggled with task management for quite some time. I have systems in place to stay on top of my emails, and while not perfect, those systems help me do massive damage to the emails that flood my inbox every day, such that I'm usually at inbox zero most days. At worst, I have less than ten emails.

I used to have trouble with my to-do list, though. I would often forget tasks, resulting in embarrassment or missed opportunities.

I have finally found a good, simple system that integrates well with my email strategy. It has helped me stay on top of everything that needs done in my writing business.

I've used just about every task management system out there: Apple Reminders, Microsoft To Do, Asana, Trello, and more. They're okay, but I would forget to use them every day, and tasks would escape me. I've also used a good old detective pad, but that's not digital and doesn't work well with my lifestyle.

I discovered that my problem wasn't finding the right app. It wasn't even remembering to check my to do list each day. It was about finding an ecosystem.

I don't like "walled gardens," and I don't like being locked into an ecosystem. But apps that work together are important when you're trying to be productive.

I've decided that for now, the Microsoft ecosystem is the best choice for me because I can integrate Outlook's calendar and email with Microsoft To Do.

Here is a description of my task management workflow and how it has helped me reach new levels of effectiveness. It is simple.

Creating Tasks

First, whenever I *create* a task, I capture it in the following format: [action verb] [task] (length of time it will take). I then assign a due date. Examples include:

- Publish *Indie Author Confidential* 12 (*45 min*)
- Fix format size on *Android Paradox* paperback and resubmit for approval at IngramSpark (15 min)
- Set up Facebook ads for *The Good Necromancer* series (1 hour)

I only assign "high priority" status to items that have a contractual obligation. Otherwise, I find high, medium, and low priorities unhelpful.

I only have three categories of to-do lists. I prefer to keep it easy:

- Follow-ups with Others
- Action Items
- Whenever

. . .

Follow-ups with Others

"Follow-ups" with others are to-dos that hold someone else accountable. Examples include:

- Confirm payment for speaking engagement (5 min)
- Follow-up with estate attorney if he does not send draft documents by October 15 (5 min)
- Marshal book links from XYZ authors for cross-promo event by June 15

In some cases, follow-ups help me ensure I receive payment for certain things like speaking events. These were the types of things that often fell through the cracks in the past.

I find that by "nudging" people early in the morning, I get best results. Therefore, I start my day with any follow-ups that need to be addressed.

Follow-ups also serve another purpose: they let the other party know that you are on top of your game. If they say they'll do something, they will find out that you will nudge them if they don't do it by the time they say they will do it. Over time, this helps to build your reputation as an effective individual, as long as you also do what you say you're going to do when you say you're going to do it.

Action Items

Mentally, I don't like to call my to do list a "to do" list. I prefer to call it a "list of action items."

The word "action" denotes, well, action.

It also reminds me of one of my first bosses, who was a highly effective individual. Whenever he needed something done, he would send an email with the words "Action item" in the subject line.

- "ACTION ITEM" denoted a task where I needed to drop everything and address, usually an angry customer.
- "Action Item" denoted a task that needed to be done, but not immediately. He would usually assign a due date in the headline as well.

While I don't follow this system with my writing business, I remember it fondly. My boss was fair, trusted me implicitly, and didn't overwhelm me with action items. In fact, he only sent a few per week.

Therefore, I call my "to do" list a list of action items instead.

I keep my action item list under ten whenever possible. Action items must *earn* a spot on the list. I used to put everything on my list, and I wondered why I was never getting anywhere. I started this year with over 50 action items and it stressed me out. Once I made a concerted effort to reduce them as much as possible, I found that my stress level dropped considerably once I got them under ten.

Action items represent only the most important tasks that will move my business forward. For all other tasks, I either don't need to do them, or I can do them whenever I remember, if I remember. It's not the end of the world either way.

Whenever

"Whenever" tasks are tasks that aren't urgent and can be done whenever I have time. This list is my task overflow. If I have more than ten tasks, excess tasks go into this list—no due date and no priority. I prioritize them whenever my action item list drops under ten.

Final Thoughts

This system is not perfect, but it works for me now, and that's all that matters. In using Microsoft Outlook and To Do integrations, I can create action items and follow-ups from emails. I don't have to worry about stringing different ecosystems together with suboptimal results.

I feel more effective than I ever have, and that's what ultimately matters. I'm sure I will continue to refine my task management efforts as time goes on, but this is a great start.

THOUGHTS ON GPT-4

GPT-4 was released on March 14, 2023 to much fanfare. This was the moment that many early adopters had been waiting for since the release of GPT-3 in 2020 and ChatGPT in 2022. This new large language model represented what many hailed as a potential new era in artificial intelligence.

I'll never forget when it launched. I was traveling and it had just woken up from a nap in a hotel room in Dallas, Texas. My social media and YouTube feeds were ablaze with people talking about the news.

My first test with GPT-4 was through ChatGPT Plus. My first impression was that it did a better job at obeying prompts and giving more detailed and interesting answers. My second impression was that it was extremely slow and at first glance not *that* different than GPT-3. Honestly, I wasn't impressed. I ran it through a gamut of tests, and the results, while better, were only marginally so. Over time, I expect the model to be refined so that it provides better results, which is the same as what happened with GPT-3. But for now, it didn't have the "wow" factor that GPT-3 had.

This was especially apparent when I used GPT-4 in my

editing application. The results were mostly the same—and in some cases significantly worse—than GPT-3. A few times, GPT-4 produced completely unusable results. The editing app did not produce *better* results or catch more errors than GPT-3.

I believe this has to do with the fact that OpenAI has transitioned from completion endpoints to chat completion endpoints. With completion endpoints, the large language model attempts to finish your prompt by guessing the next word. With a chat completion, the large language model thinks you are trying to chat, and its answers are based on that assumption, leading to strange outputs when you ask it to merely proofread text. It gets confused when you're not trying to chat.

I'm not a fan of the chat completion endpoint, and I strongly believe that when we look back on the progression of the GPT large language models, the abandonment of straight completion endpoints will be a notable mistake. People are so infatuated with "chatting" with large language models, but there are so many other uses. At some point, people will get tired of ChatGPT because there will be other ways to interface with large language models that are more efficient and fit people's digital lifestyles better. If you think about it, it takes a lot of effort to sit down and chat with a large language model. To do this, it is assumed that you can type moderately well, phrase your prompts with a modicum of skill, and, if the result is not what you need, try again. It's a lot of friction, and when we look back on this moment several years from now, people will say "We used to chat with AI like that? How savage!"

In any case, while GPT-4 is a step forward in many respects, it is a major step backward for editing. But sometimes, that's how life goes. This is what progress looks and feels like.

LOOKING FORWARD

BOOK OF THE MONTH MARKETING

I was talking to a friend. She is a successful author and speaker, and she is very organized.

She was telling me about her marketing strategy, which is to focus on one book a month. She picks a book, discounts it for one weekend, runs advertisements, promotes it to her audience and e-mail newsletter, and other tasks that are part and parcel to marketing and promotion. She says it's helpful for her to have a monthly marketing cadence.

I liked the idea a lot. After all, I have nearly 100 books and I could benefit from such a strategy. If there's anything I don't do on a regular basis, it's marketing. I'm a big fan of "set it and forget it" or "set it and tweak it on occasion" types of marketing. They just suit my busy lifestyle better.

But, I could manage one book a month for marketing, no problem. Out of my catalog of books, I have approximately 40 or so that I could market. These are book ones and standalones.

If I can ever get my act together, I will try this strategy. I'm recording it here so that I can enter it into my subconscious and be ready for it when the time comes.

BEATING PARKINSON'S LAW

This quarter, I benefited from beating Parkinson's Law. Not to be confused with Parkinson's Disease, this law governs productivity and, by proxy, procrastination.

Parkinson's Law states that work expands to fill the time available for its completion. This law was first proposed by Cyril Northcote Parkinson in 1955, based on his observations of bureaucracy and organizational behavior. While Parkinson's law is widely cited, it is important to note that it is not a universally applicable law and may not hold true in all situations.

But boy, does it hold true for writers. If a writer is given a deadline of October 1st to finish a manuscript, that manuscript won't be done until 11:59 PM on September 30th. This isn't because the writer is lazy; it's because of Parkinson's Law. I have striven to beat Parkinson's Law in my life wherever and whenever possible. If someone gives me six months to complete something, I try to finish it in three. Why? Because the sooner you finish something, the less stress it gives you. I don't have any way to prove this, but I'm certain that all those tasks with distant deadlines linger on your subconscious and add stress to you even when you don't realize it. That has certainly been the case for me, hence why I like to beat Parkinson's Law whenever possible.

This was especially helpful earlier this year. I signed a contract with Writer's Digest to produce six webinars on various topics related to writing and publishing. They gave me an extremely generous deadline of 18 months from the date I signed the contract. I had this time to prepare PowerPoint presentations, record them, edit them, send them to the Writer's Digest team, and so on.

Most people would put off these webinars until a few weeks before they were due. After all, why even spend time thinking about something that's due a year and a half from today?

That's not an incorrect way to approach things in life. In fact, there is virtue in waiting to do tasks; for example, you may not have enough information to complete a task, or the circumstances around completing that task may change drastically over a long period of time. I can tell you that in corporate America, I do not strive to beat Parkinson's Law except in rare circumstances (like getting work done before a vacation or before another big project is slated to start). The sands of corporate America shift far too often to even think about beating Parkinson's Law. But in my writing life, I beat the hell out of Parkinson's Law all the time.

I finished the webinars within three months. I took my time and executed them to the best of my ability. I believe I did a better job than if I would have waited until a few weeks before the deadline.

Most importantly, I completed the last of the webinars shortly before contracting mold poisoning, so while I was dealing with the illness, the webinars were *not* on my mind, which aided my recovery.

That's why I love beating Parkinson's Law. Sometimes, it can really help you out.

SPEAKING WHILE ON THE ROAD

I found myself in the unfortunate situation of having to perform a contractually obligated speaking engagement while on the road. My wife had to travel on short notice to Dallas, Texas, and I overlooked my engagement on my calendar. Even worse, I forgot that I had to host a podcast episode of the *Self-Publishing Advice & Inspirations Podcast*, and I couldn't find a stand-in substitute at such short notice.

I pride myself on providing the best speaking experience that I can, and doing so from a hotel room with my laptop's built-in microphone just wasn't going to cut it. Yet, I had signed a contract and I had to show up because the event was being advertised to hundreds of participants.

Fortunately, Dallas is a cool city. I found a co-working space where I paid a modest fee to use the facilities for the day. This co-working space was unique because it had a podcast studio!

It must have been God looking out for me because the studio had acoustic foam on the walls, a mixer, and even the same microphone that I used to have at home: the Audio-Technica AT-2035. I know this microphone extremely well and how to operate it. I did a dry run with the equipment, and when the fateful day came, I used the equipment to great effect. In fact, the engagement is on YouTube, and I will reference it in the "Content Created While Writing This Book" section. You can judge the results for yourself.

For the podcast episode, I wasn't so lucky, and I failed epically. I purchased a Samson Go microphone that arrived at my house the day before I was scheduled to fly to Dallas. It would have been a good substitute for my laptop's built-in equipment, but I was never able to test it because I left the connection cable at home, therefore rendering it useless. Needless to say, the podcast episode sounded god-awful, and it was embarrassing. I will also reference it at the back of this book for grins and giggles.

In any case, sometimes huge wins are followed almost immediately by huge losses, and vice versa. That's life.

Despite the epic fail, if the Samson Go microphone works well in the future, I took a big step forward in being able to give dynamic and professional speaking engagements from the road if I ever need to do this in the future.

DEVELOPING A MICROSOFT WORD COURSE

I received an opportunity to speak at this year's annual Writer's Digest Conference. One of my talks was about Microsoft Word.

In a previous volume in the series, I discussed being blown away by just how many people attended a talk on basic Microsoft Word tips at a recent writing conference. The room was packed. Since I specialize in writing up tutorials, I thought it would be an interesting idea to try this for myself and in my own style.

I titled the talk "Microsoft Word Unleashed." I wanted to focus on basic but powerful tips that writers can use every day in Microsoft Word. Nothing complicated, nothing fancy--just useful, practical tips. I made a list of every tip I could think of, which ended at around 75. There was no way I could teach 75 tips in an hour-long talk, so I narrowed the list to 11. My criteria were that they had to be simple, common, practical, and something someone would use frequently.

Here's the refined list:

1. Auto save
2. Dark mode

3. Snap assist (Windows) and Split View (Mac)
4. Task switching
5. Smart pasting
6. Clipboard manager
7. Format painter
8. Compare and combine
9. Advanced find and replace
10. Find by formatting
11. Tracked changes

I also included some miscellaneous tips interspersed with the list above, but you get the picture.

Next, I had to figure out how to teach these features. My understanding was that the venue room would be quite large. Even though there were screens, it would be hard for participants to see the finer details.

So, I came up with two cockamamie ideas:

1. Stream my screen to participants' laptops, with a replay of the talk available afterward.
2. Create a course with the same content as a resource to use later.

We'll take them one at a time.

I expect many people to bring their laptops to an event like this, so why not follow along? If they can watch on their screens, that would solve all of my problems.

I hatched an elaborate scheme to accomplish this task. I confirmed with the event organizer that the following strategy would be okay because it was out-of-the-box.

I would use StreamYard (a streaming platform) to share my

screen. I would stream to YouTube and give the participants a simple link so that they could watch easily. Yes, I know that this is technical, but anyone can open a browser and visit a simple link such as www.authorlevelup.com/watch. Those without laptops could also watch on their phones, so I would include a QR code for them.

The only point of weakness would be the hotel Wi-Fi. I would be completely at its mercy. If it didn't work, the whole plan would fall apart. If this happened, I would fall back on my second strategy, which I also planned to implement.

The second part of my plan involved creating a professional Microsoft Word course on Teachable. I would cover all the tips that I would hit in my presentation. Each video of the course would be no longer than five minutes. I would put the maximum effort into it to make it a premium course worth paying for. I would then give the course away to participants as a final gift via a coupon code. (Plus, I can sell this course in the future)

This way, if the streaming didn't work, they would have access to substantially the same content with high production value. And, I could say at the beginning of the presentation that if they can't see the screen, there would be 1) a replay of my screen available immediately after the conclusion of the presentation and 2) a premium course that covers everything in my talk (and more).

Will it work? I'm not sure. I haven't given the talk at the time of this writing, but I am ready. I will include a follow-up chapter in the next volume of the series to report on whether it was a success or a failure.

CONTENT CREATED WHILE WRITING THIS BOOK

This section recaps the books I've published and media I've created during the quarter. To keep the book evergreen, I will not include links to podcasts or magazine articles because sometimes links break over time, especially with podcasts if the hosts stop podcasting. You can easily search for them to see if they're still active at the time you're reading this book. If they are, enjoy! If not, please accept my apologies.

Magazine Articles

"Editing with GPT." *Indie Author Magazine.* An article on the benefits of AI for editing. April 7, 2023.

READ THE NEXT VOLUME

Michael's writer journey continues in the next volume of this series!

Grab your copy at www.authorlevelup.com/confidential.

MEET M.L. RONN

Science fiction and fantasy on the wild side!

M.L. Ronn (Michael La Ronn) is the author of many science fiction and fantasy novels including *The Good Necromancer, Android X,* and *The Last Dragon Lord* series.

In 2012, a life-threatening illness made him realize that storytelling was his #1 passion. He's devoted his life to writing ever since, making up whatever story makes him fall out of his chair laughing the hardest. Every day.

Learn more about Michael
www.authorlevelup.com (for writers)
www.michaellaronn.com (fiction)

MORE BOOKS BY M.L. RONN

Books for Writers:

www.authorlevelup.com/books

Fiction:
www.michaellaronn.com/books